To Matilda, with love xx
V.F.

To Caroline, with much love
A.B.

OLIVER'S MILKSHAKE
First edition published in 2000
by Hodder Children's Books

Text copyright © Vivian French 2000
Illustrations copyright © Alison Bartlett 2000

Hodder Children's Books
338 Euston Road
London, NW1 3BH

Hodder Children's Books Australia
Level 17/207 Kent Street
Sydney, NSW 2000

ISBN: 978 0 340 75454 2

Printed in China.

Hodder Children's Books is a division of Hachette Children's Books.
An Hachette Livre UK Company.
www.hachettelivre.co.uk

Oliver's Milkshake

Vivian French

Illustrated by
Alison Bartlett

Hodder Children's Books

A division of Hachette Children's Books

Mum woke Oliver at eight o'clock.
'Time to get up!' she said. 'Remember you're going out
for the day with Auntie Jen and Lily.'
    'Do I have to?' asked Oliver.
    'Yes,' said Mum. 'I'm going shopping.'
    'Oh,' said Oliver. 'I hate shopping.'

Auntie Jen bustled in just after half-past nine.
'Goodness me, Oliver,' she said. 'Orange squash
for breakfast? Milk is MUCH better for your
teeth and bones!'
Lily made a face.

'I don't . . .' began Oliver.
'You don't like milk!' Auntie Jen
wagged a finger at him.
'Just like my Lily. What YOU need is
one of my yummy milkshakes.'

The town clock struck ten as they drove past.

'Where are we going?' asked Oliver.
'Shopping!' said Auntie Jen.
Lily sighed loudly. Oliver looked horrified.
'But Mum said we were going out for the day!'
'We are,' beamed Auntie Jen. 'We're
going out shopping for a yummy
scrummy milkshake.'

Oliver *was* surprised when Auntie Jen parked the car.
'Out you hop!' she said cheerfully.
'There aren't any shops here,' said Oliver. 'Only fields.'
'That's right,' she nodded. 'We're going to a farm.
We're going to buy fresh milk from real cows, and fresh fruit.
Then we'll go home again, and what'll we do then?'

Oliver looked hopeful.
'Watch a video?'
'No!' said Auntie Jen.
'We'll make a yummy scrummy
fruity milkshake!'
'Oh,' said Oliver.

Oliver climbed on the fence
and a big woolly sheep looked up.
'Baa,' it said loudly. 'Baaaa!'
Lily giggled. 'It's asking you if you want
a scritchy scratchy puffy fluffy woolly jumper!'
'No, thanks,' Oliver said. 'Tell it I'm going to
have a yummy scrummy fruity fluffy milkshake.'
'Frothy,' said Lily, 'not fluffy!'

Lots of hens were strutting and scratching
about in the yard.
'Cluck!' they said. 'Cluck! Cluck! Cluck!'
'Do you put eggs in milkshakes?' Oliver asked.
'Goodness me, no!' said Auntie Jen.
'Oh,' said Oliver. 'I just wondered.'
'No yolky joky eggs,' said Lily. 'Not in our
yummy scrummy fruity frothy icy milkshake.'

'OINK! OINK!'
Oliver jumped. 'What's that?'
Auntie Jen laughed loudly. 'Pigs, Oliver. Just there!'
Oliver and Lily stared into the pig pen.
'Wow!' said Oliver. 'She's huge!'
Lily was counting. 'Eight . . . nine . . . ten piglets!'
'And they're drinking their milk like good
little piglets,' said Auntie Jen.
Oliver and Lily looked at each other.
'But they're not drinking yummy
scrummy fruity frothy
icy nicy milkshakes!'

Lily got bored of watching the piglets.
She peeped over the open-top door of a shed.
'Goats!' she said.
Oliver came to see and so did Auntie Jen.
'Goat's milk is delicious,' Auntie Jen told Oliver.
'Yuck!' said Lily. 'I HATE goat's milk.'
'Nonsense, Lily,' Auntie Jen frowned.
'You've never even tried it.'

Oliver saw the cows first.
They were big . . . much bigger than Oliver.
'There!' said Auntie Jen. 'Aren't they wonderful?
You stay here and look at them and I'll go
and buy our special creamy milk.'
Oliver felt a little anxious.
'Can I come with you?' he asked.
'I'm coming too,' said Lily.

In the farm shop Auntie Jen
bought a big carton of fresh milk.
'Oliver dear, what's your favourite
fruit?' she asked.
'Blueberries,' Oliver said.
'Then we'll buy blueberries for our
milkshake,' smiled Auntie Jen.
Lily nodded. 'Our yummy
scrummy fruity frothy icy nicy . . .
what was the next bit, Oliver?'
Oliver beamed. 'Tip top tasty!'

'Mum!' Oliver rushed into the kitchen. 'We're back! And Auntie Jen is going to make a yummy scrummy fruity frothy icy nicy tip top tasty DREAMY CREAMY milkshake.'
'I certainly am,' said Auntie Jen. 'This young man needs his milk.'
She pulled out Mum's mixer and tipped in the milk and the blueberries. Then she chopped up a banana and dropped that in too.

WHRRRRRRRRRRRRRRR

The mixer whizzed and whirred.
'You'll love this!' said Auntie Jen.
'Mmm,' said Oliver.
'This is scrumptious!'

Oliver finished his milkshake with
a loud slurp.
　'Mum,' he said, 'can I have
one of these tonight
instead of my hot milk?'

Auntie Jen stared at him. 'But, Oliver,' she said, 'you don't like milk!'
'Yes I do!' Oliver said indignantly. 'I only had orange squash for breakfast today because I put too much milk on my cornflakes. There wasn't any left to drink!'